THINGS WE WEAR

SOME OTHER BOOKS BY VARDELL & WONG

Things We Do

Things We Eat

Things We Feel

*Hop to It:
Poems to Get You Moving*

*Pet Crazy:
A Poetry Friday Power Book*

*The Poetry Friday Anthology
for Celebrations*

The Poetry of Science

THINGS
WE
WEAR

by
Sylvia Vardell & Janet Wong

Pomelo
Books

**100% of the profits from this book
will be donated
to the IBBY Children in Crisis Fund**

IBBY CHILDREN IN CRISIS
The IBBY Children in Crisis Fund provides support for children whose lives have been disrupted through war, civil disorder, or natural disaster. The program gives immediate support and help — and also aims for long-term community impact, aligning with IBBY's goal of giving every child the right to become a reader.

ibby.org/awards-activities/ibby-children-in-crisis-fund
usbby.org/donate.html

Special thanks to Renée M. LaTulippe for her ongoing help in editing Pomelo Books publications.

No part of this publication may be reproduced, or stored in a retrieval system, or transmitted in any form or by any means, electronic, mechanical, photocopying, recording, or otherwise, without written permission of the publisher. For information regarding permission, please contact us:

Pomelo Books
9440 Viewside Dr
Dallas TX 75231
PomeloBooks.com
info@pomelobooks.com

Text/compilation copyright © 2022 by Pomelo Books. All rights reserved.
Individual poems copyright © 2022 by the individual poets. All rights reserved.
Photos sourced from Canva.com.

Library of Congress Cataloging-in-Publication Data is available.
ISBN 978-1-937057-04-6

Please visit us:
PomeloBooks.com

POEMS BY

Robyn Hood Black
Willeena Booker
Sandy Brehl
Judy Bryan
Rose Cappelli
Janet Clare Fagal
Karen Elise Finch
Douglas Florian
Patricia J. Franz
Theresa Gaughan
Xelena González
Katey Howes
Molly Lorenz

Amy Milholland
Moe Phillips
Donna JT Smith
Holly Thompson
Linda Kulp Trout
Fernanda Valentino
Amy Ludwig VanDerwater
Padma Venkatraman
Jenna Waldman
Vicki Wilke
Matthew Winter
Janet Wong
Helen Kemp Zax

TABLE OF CONTENTS

APRON	by Matthew Winter	9
BOOTS	by Jenna Waldman	11
COSTUME	by Donna JT Smith	13
DRESS	by Xelena González	15
EARMUFFS	by Patricia J. Franz	17
FLIP-FLOPS	by Willeena Booker	19
GLASSES	by Vicki Wilke	21
HELMET	by Amy Milholland	23
ICE SKATES	by Janet Clare Fagal	25
JEANS	by Moe Phillips	27
KIPPAH	by Douglas Florian	29
LIFE JACKET	by Theresa Gaughan	31
MASK	by Sandy Brehl	33
NECKLACE	by Linda Kulp Trout	35
OVERALLS	by Katey Howes	37
PAJAMAS	by Helen Kemp Zax	39
QUILT	by Molly Lorenz	41
RAINCOAT	by Rose Cappelli	43

SARI	by Padma Venkatraman	45
T-SHIRT	by Janet Wong	47
UNIFORM	by Amy Ludwig VanDerwater	49
VISOR	by Fernanda Valentino	51
WATCH	by Robyn Hood Black	53
X-RAY APRON	by Judy Bryan	55
YUKATA	by Holly Thompson	57
ZIPPER	by Karen Elise Finch	59
ALPHABET CLOTHES	by Janet Wong	61
Resources for Parents and Teachers		63
Tips for Readers		64
Fun Activities to Try		66
Web Resources		68
About the Poets		70
Poem Credits		74
About Vardell & Wong		76
About Pomelo Books		77
Other Books by Vardell & Wong		78

APRON

by Matthew Winter

A dot
A fleck
A splotch
A splatter

A blot
A speck
A blotch
No matter

An apron protects
from any spot –
spill a little
or spill a LOT!

BOOTS

by Jenna Waldman

I'm never taking off my boots,
they'll never leave my feet!
I'll wear them when I brush my teeth,
I'll wear them when I eat.

I'm never taking off my boots,
no matter what the weather.
And when I nap, then they'll nap too.
We'll always be together!

COSTUME

by Donna JT Smith

This is my costume.
It isn't for play.
I swoop and leap,
saving the day!

No one can know
who's in this mask
doing good things.
"Who's that?" they ask.

If you knew it was me
you'd say, "You're a kid!"
and wouldn't believe
what this superkid did!

DRESS

by Xelena González

Let the colors
blooming inside you
soar out to meet the rest
with a smile and a swirl
of your best dancing dress!

EARMUFFS

by Patricia J. Franz

Bundle up to play outside.

Find your winter gear!

Boots and scarves and earmuffs . . .

Wait!

Snowmen don't have ears!

FLIP-FLOPS

by Willeena Booker

I love to wear my flip-flops
I have a favorite pair
they fit snug against my feet
my toes feel free in soft warm air

I wear them to the beach
and the sand tickles my feet
I sit and swing them back and forth
in the sweet summer heat

GLASSES

by Vicki Wilke

Rows and rows of glasses.
Which ones will we choose?
We try them on, we put them back —
metallics, browns, and blues.

We must have tried a hundred,
before we found "just right."
My sister picked flamingo pink,
and I chose pearly white.

Mama's frames are solid black.
They make her look so wise.
Look here, everybody —
smile with your eyes!

HELMET

by Amy Milholland

I'm learning how to ride my bike.
My dad puts a **helmet** on me.

I hope I don't fall, but if I do,
my dad's right here to protect me.

I look back. Where'd he go?
He's standing way behind me.

Am I pedaling on my own now?
I am pedaling on my own now!

I hope I don't fall, but if I do,
my **helmet**'s right here to protect me.

ICE SKATES

by Janet Clare Fagal

At the rink, it's time to skate.
I'm new at this but I can't wait!
I glide a bit, then stop. And stumble.
My helmet's on, in case I tumble.

Holding hands, we're off once more.
I'm moving better than before!
My new **ice skates** feel nice and tight.
I know I'll skate my best tonight.

JEANS

by Moe Phillips

Our jeans are hip!
Our jeans are cool!
Sometimes I wear
my jeans to school.
Our jeans are blue!
Blue like the sea.
We're a blue jean family!

KIPPAH

by Douglas Florian

I keep my kippah on my head
until it's time to go to bed.
It shows how much I love Hashem.
And it reminds me who I am.
I'm proud to be a Jew, you see.
That's what my kippah means to me.

Note: The word *Hashem* is another way of saying God.

LIFE JACKET

by Theresa Gaughan

When we're on the boat,
we watch egrets fly.
We spot turtles on logs.
We watch fish swim by.

When we leave the dock
to sail out on the lake,
I wear my life jacket,
so I'm always safe.

MASK

by Sandy Brehl

What's behind my mask?
Just ask!

One missing tooth,
two dimples,
three freckles,
more giggles,
kind smiles.

Behind my mask,
it's me —
your friend!

NECKLACE

by Linda Kulp Trout

Grandma wants a necklace
but not one from a store.
She says homemade gifts
always mean much more.

So I made her a necklace.
(I know she'll be surprised!)
I can't wait to see
the *happy* in Grandma's eyes.

OVERALLS

by Katey Howes

I put on brand new overalls
this morning when I dressed.
I haven't had a pair before.
I'm overall impressed.
My clothes need lots of pockets.
Pants with pockets pass my test.
I wear a few with only two
and four in all the rest,
but overalls have FIVE!
The biggest one is on the chest.
A perfect place to tuck and store
the items I like best.

PAJAMAS

by Helen Kemp Zax

Do you ever let your puppy
lie beside you on your bed?
Do his whiskers tick-tick-tickle
as he snuggles by your head?

Do you dress him in **pajamas**?
Do you hear his heartbeat beat?
Do you hold him as he chases
squirrels on dreaming doggy feet?

Do you love him as you fall asleep
and love him while you're sleeping?
Do you promise to take care of him
for always and for keeping?

QUILT

by Molly Lorenz

She sewed this quilt
from patches of cloth.
I wrap it tightly
around me.

Cozy and warm
when I'm feeling cold.
Grandma's love
surrounds me.

RAINCOAT

by Rose Cappelli

My raincoat pops with polka dots –
yellow, pink, and red.
So rain drip-drops on polka dots
instead of on my head!

SARI

by Padma Venkatraman

"There's more than a hundred ways
to tie a *sari*," Grandma says.
Maybe so, but I know
there's only one way to wear a *sari*:
with a proud and happy smile!

T-SHIRT

by Janet Wong

When I wear my chess club T-shirt,
it helps me think better.

I love my chess club T-shirt,
every single piece and letter.

My chess club T-shirt tells you
that I'm part of this club.

What T-shirts do you have
that show the things you love?

UNIFORM

by Amy Ludwig VanDerwater

A uniform is what we wear
to look a bit the same
when we go to school
or play a soccer game.
Inside we are different.
Outside we both wear blue.
Are you matching me
or am I matching you?

VISOR

by Fernanda Valentino

I'm not a beanie
I'm not a hat
I'm more like half a baseball cap . . .
My wide brim shields you from the sun
I am a visor . . .
Let's go have FUN!

WATCH

by Robyn Hood Black

Skinny hands
move on its face
second by second – tick, tick.

A clock with a band
always in place
never too slow or too quick, quick.

There isn't a buzz
a beep or a chime
but watching my watch –
I can tell time!

X-RAY APRON

by Judy Bryan

When Pumpkin hurt her leg,
she needed an exam.
We rushed her to the vet –
our favorite Dr. Sam.

I wore an x-ray apron
to keep my bones protected
from radiation waves
while Pumpkin was inspected.

The vet said, "Nothing's broken.
Good news! But two things, please –
she'll need some extra love,
and no more climbing trees!"

YUKATA

by Holly Thompson

Find your yukata,
get ready to go.
Put right side to left hip,
left side to right.
Wrap the long obi
and tie in a bow
Slip feet into sandals –
it's festival night!

ZIPPER

by Karen Elise Finch

I can do it!
Don't need help!

Well, maybe . . .
just a little start?

My zipper pieces
are apart.

Thank you!
There! See my grin?

My zipper now
is by my chin!

A B C D E F G
H I J K
L M N O P
Q R S T U V
W X Y Z

ALPHABET CLOTHES

by Janet Wong

Britney's backpack says her name,
BRITNEY, in bright blue thread.
Alex has a monogrammed shirt
that shows his name in red.

We don't have money for things like that,
but Grandma takes care of my clothes.
She writes my initials in marker
so everybody knows:

That's my jacket in the lost and found.
This is my sweater on the table.
Grandma made alphabet clothes for me
with permanent love on the label.

RESOURCES FOR PARENTS & TEACHERS

TIPS FOR READERS

Here are some basic strategies for sharing poetry with children. Whether you're a family member, caregiver, teacher, librarian, or school administrator, these tips will help you get kids excited about reading!

Reading the pictures
With very young children, reading begins with everything EXCEPT the words. Encourage children to "read" or interpret the pictures and talk about what they see. Help them name the clothing items pictured. Which are familiar items and which are new? Which words are familiar and which are new?

Reading aloud
Even if your child can read independently, it's good to hear poems read aloud for their sound qualities. Poems are meant to be read out loud to savor the words, sounds, and rhythm. Plus, reading aloud together is a bonding time that makes reading a positive experience for young children just beginning to master the skills of reading.

Props and pantomime
Whether you're reading to a group of children or just one child, simple props or pantomime can make your read-aloud come alive. Are you wearing any of the following items featured in the poems: GLASSES, JEANS, MASK, NECKLACE, or ZIPPER? If so, point them out as you read the accompanying poem out loud.

Combine listening and reading with echo reading
With echo reading, a child or a group of children will repeat lines of a poem after hearing you read them. Pause after each line and put a hand to your ear to cue your readers to repeat what they've just heard.

Point to words
Pointing to words as you read them is a great way to help children learn to read and helps them begin to associate the spoken word with the written word. It also reinforces the concept that English text moves from left to right, top to bottom.

Encourage guessing
Children often like rhyming poems because it's easy to guess the words that come at regular rhyming intervals. They sometimes will guess the wrong words, but it's good to encourage guessing; it makes reading feel like a game and builds prediction skills essential to comprehension.

Read parts
Some poems have a repeated word or phrase that you can point out before you start reading. You can read just the line with those repeated words before you read the whole poem. Children can join in when they hear those repeated words or phrases.

Read, respond, and be open
Talking about our feelings is an important part of processing those feelings and poems can help us do that. As you read these poems aloud, be open to children's responses; they often notice surprising things and make interesting connections. It's also fine just to read a poem and move on.

Record the reading
Record a poem to share with a friend or family member far away. It's easy to make an audio or video recording of a child reading either alone or together with you; simply use your phone or an online tool like Zoom or Google Meet. Or record yourself reading for your child to enjoy later when you may be away.

FUN ACTIVITIES TO TRY

Here are some activities for having fun with poetry in more creative ways after you've read and shared each poem.

Poem titles
Each poem has a one-word title and that word also appears in the poem itself in a different color. This makes it easy for children to join in on that key word as you read the rest of the poem aloud and point to the word when it's their turn.

Learning letters
After reading the poem aloud, challenge children to think of other words that start with the same initial letter. For example, for A = APRON, you might offer *apple, alligator, art,* etc. For B = BOOTS, you might offer *belt, bandana, bathrobe*, and so on.

Number words
Many of the poems in this book include number words, such as GLASSES, MASK, OVERALLS, SARI, and WATCH. After reading the poem together, identify the number words and talk about how poems can use both words and numbers.

Time for poetry
Reading a poem out loud takes less than a minute! Add a quick poem to your routine to build incidental literacy development. Start the day with a poem at breakfast, copy and add a poem to a lunch bag, or end the day with a poem read at dinner or at bedtime. Commemorate the first day of school with a poem, or the last day of school, or "moving up" day. You can also share a poem to celebrate a birthday.

Translate
Translate your favorite poem into another language spoken in your family or community. You can work with a friend or a neighbor or try GoogleTranslate to see how your poem sounds in French or Chinese or another language.

Poems in parts
Several poems in this book use italics, quotation marks, or all capital letters for key words or phrases. As you read the poem aloud, cue children to join in on the word or phrase in italics, quotes, or capitals in the poems APRON, OVERALLS, T-SHIRT, VISOR (capitals); NECKLACE (italics); COSTUME, SARI, and X-RAY APRON (quotation marks).

Body parts and movement
Many of the poems in this book refer to body parts and movement within the poem, such as *eyes, ears, heads, arms,* and *feet*. Invite children to point to each body part as you read the poem out loud or act out the motions described in the poem.

Family poems
Several poems are about moments we share with our families and pets. Work with children to share poems with their families, especially JEANS, as well as HELMET (referring to fathers), GLASSES (referring to mothers), NECKLACE, QUILT, or SARI referring to grandmothers, and even PAJAMAS with a pet dog or X-RAY APRON with a pet cat!

Types of poems
There are several different types of poems in this book, some rhyming like APRON, ICE SKATES, and QUILT, and some free verse or non-rhyming like MASK. Some poems use repetition (BOOTS, JEANS) and some use questions (PAJAMAS, HELMET). Challenge children to try creating a poem using one of these elements.

WEB RESOURCES

There are so many useful literacy resources online that it's sometimes hard to know where to start. You'll find basic information and engaging activities at the following recommended websites. Dive in and have fun!

childfun.com/themes/people/clothes/
Try these fun and engaging arts and crafts activities, games, songs, poems, and finger plays all related to the topic of clothing for young children.

childmind.org
The Child Mind Institute is a research-based resource for families and caregivers on mental health and brain development. Accessible in both English and Spanish.

cradlestocrayons.org
Cradles to Crayons works to end clothing insecurity by providing free clothing to children in need by connecting community organizations with their Giving Factory warehouse.

colorincolorado.org
Colorín Colorado is a national multimedia project that offers bilingual activities and advice for educators and families of English language learners (ELLs).

everychildareader.net
Every Child a Reader connects book creators with learning communities, providing literacy tools and resources. Their many outreach programs include the Kids' Book Choice Awards.

healthiergeneration.org
Alliance for a Healthier Generation works with schools, youth organizations, and businesses to support children's physical and social-emotional health.

healthline.com/health/childrens-health/playing-dress-up
Imaginative dress-up play has many benefits for child development. Find tips and ideas for getting started here.

ibby.org
The International Board on Books for Young People (IBBY) is an international network with dozens of chapters all over the world working together to connect children with books.

naeyc.org
The National Association for the Education of Young Children (NAEYC) is a membership organization that provides professional development and support for early childhood educators and families.

reachoutandread.org
Endorsed by the American Academy of Pediatrics (AAP), this site provides early literacy tools in Spanish, screen-free activities, and links to even more resources for reading with children.

usbby.org
The United States Board on Books for Young People (USBBY) is the U.S. national section of IBBY, with an Outstanding International Books List that features titles for children that promote global understanding.

ABOUT THE POETS

You probably found some favorite poems when reading this book. Write down the poets' names and learn more about them by visiting their websites and blogs. Then look for more of their poems (and books)!

Robyn Hood Black   robynhoodblack.com
Robyn Hood Black makes poems and art in South Carolina. She loves fancy old watch faces and antique clock parts. Her favorite way to spend time is being with her family.

Willeena Booker   Twitter: @WilleenaB
Willeena Booker is an educator, poet, and advocate of social justice. Her work appears in *Things We Feel* and *What Is a Friend?* by Pomelo Books. Willeena loves flip-flopping around writing poems!

Sandy Brehl   sandybrehlbooks.com
Sandy Brehl writes poems, picture books, verse novels, and prose novels. When she's not writing, she's READING! Under her mask are two dimples, MANY freckles, and a friendly smile.

Judy Bryan   judybryanauthor.com
Judy Bryan wears many hats including children's book author, reader, poet, and pet wrangler. She is thankful the only x-ray apron she's had to wear was at the dentist's office!

Rose Cappelli   imaginethepossibilitiesblog.wordpress.com
Rose Cappelli enjoys sharing her love of language and story in her poems and picture books. She has lots of coats, but not a raincoat with polka dots . . . yet.

Janet Clare Fagal   Facebook: facebook.com/janet.clare.311
Janet Clare Fagal's poems appear in five Pomelo anthologies, among others, and at nlapw.org. When a kind ten-year-old named Joe Murray lent her a hand, she finally learned to skate – even backwards!

Karen Elise Finch   Twitter: @nestofbooks
Karen Elise Finch has shared her love of words and images as a preschool teacher, art educator, and library assistant. She lives in Michigan, the "mitten state," with her zipper often by her chin.

Douglas Florian   douglasflorian.com
Douglas Florian is an artist and author of many acclaimed picture book poetry collections he has both written and illustrated, like *Zoobilations!* He is a native New Yorker who is constantly inspired by nature and occasionally wears a kippah.

Patricia J. Franz   patriciajfranz.com
Patricia J. Franz writes poetry and picture books. Her poems have appeared in the anthologies *Things We Feel* and *What Is a Friend?* and she wears fuzzy red earmuffs in winter!

Theresa Gaughan   Twitter: @TheresaGaughan
Theresa Gaughan is a veteran teacher who enjoys writing and sharing poetry with her third-grade students. She wears a life jacket while kayaking on a lake near her home.

Xelena González   xelena.space
Xelena González is the award-winning author of *All Around Us*, *Where Wonder Grows*, and *Remembering*. Her favorite dress to wear to school visits features 90 cats wearing glasses.

Katey Howes   kateyhowes.com
Katey Howes is the author of numerous picture books, including *A Poem Grows Inside You*. Katey works to give kids an overall sense of agency and innovation - and a deep love of reading.

Molly Lorenz   Twitter: @booksR4me
Molly Lorenz is a member of SCBWI and a retired art teacher. She has been published in *Things We Do* and *What Is a Friend?* She enjoys painting and creating warm and cozy quilts from patches of cloth.

Amy Milholland   amymilholland.com
Amy Milholland is a writer and artist who enjoyed riding her bike as a kid. Although she doesn't ride as much anymore, she relies on her helmet to protect her when she does.

Moe Phillips   moephillips.com
Poet and filmmaker Moe Phillips loves anything magical. Over 30 of her poems and essays have appeared in anthologies and magazines for children and adults. Find Moe writing in her blue jeans!

Donna JT Smith   mainelywrite.blogspot.com
Donna lives by the ocean. She loves books. If she sits under a sheet, she can read all day! Everyone thinks she's a ghost and stays away! It's her favorite costume!

Holly Thompson   hatbooks.com
Holly Thompson, from Massachusetts, has lived in Japan for many years. She writes books for young people, teaches at Yokohama City University, and presents at schools worldwide. She loves wearing yukata at summer festivals.

Linda Kulp Trout   lindakulptrout.blogspot.com
Linda Kulp Trout writes poetry for children. Her poems have appeared in anthologies, teacher resources, and magazines. When she is not writing, she enjoys making homemade gifts for her family and friends.

Fernanda Valentino   Twitter: @fgvalentino
Fernanda Valentino was born and raised in Perth, Australia, and now lives in Chicago. She loves having fun and since she doesn't have one, she will be on the lookout for a handy-dandy visor!

Amy Ludwig VanDerwater   amyludwigvanderwater.com
Amy Ludwig VanDerwater loves making things, writes books for children, blogs at The Poem Farm, and lives in the country. As a little girl, she wore a plaid skirt as part of her school uniform.

Padma Venkatraman   padmavenkatraman.com
Padma Venkatraman worked as chief scientist on research vessels before becoming the author of novels such as *The Bridge Home* and *Born Behind Bars*. Her two favorite things to wear for special occasions are a sari – and a happy smile!

Jenna Waldman   jennawaldman.com
Jenna Waldman is the author of several picture books including *Larry's Latkes* and *Sharkbot Shalom*. She hopes her writing fuels her readers' creativity – and perhaps they'll become writers to boot!

Vicki Wilke   winningwriters.com/people/vicki-wilke
Vicki Wilke joyfully taught K-1 for 33 years, while writing and publishing poetry for all ages. Five precious grandchildren fill her with poetry inspiration – and while writing, glasses are always perched on her nose!

Matthew Winter   Twitter: @Baileysdad420
Matthew Winter is a first-grade teacher in New York. He loves writing poems and baking. He always wears an apron when he bakes confections in the kitchen with his poodle-son, Bailey.

Helen Kemp Zax   helenzax.com
Helen Kemp Zax is a former lawyer whose poems have been published in anthologies such as *HOP TO IT: Poems to Get You Moving* and *Imperfect II*. Every morning Helen writes poetry with her dog Huck at her feet – although only she is wearing pajamas.

POEM CREDITS

These poems are used with the permission of the individual authors, with all rights reserved. To request reprint rights, please send an email to info@pomelobooks.com and we'll connect you with the poets.

Robyn Hood Black: "WATCH"; © 2022 by Robyn Hood Black.

Willeena Booker: "FLIP-FLOPS"; © 2022 by Willeena Booker.

Sandy Brehl: "MASK"; © 2022 by Sandy Brehl.

Judy Bryan: "X-RAY APRON"; © 2022 by Judy Bryan.

Rose Cappelli: "RAINCOAT"; © 2022 by Rose Cappelli.

Janet Clare Fagal: "ICE SKATES"; © 2022 by Janet Clare Fagal.

Karen Elise Finch: "ZIPPER"; © 2022 by Karen Elise Finch.

Douglas Florian: "KIPPAH"; © 2022 by Douglas Florian.

Patricia J. Franz: "EARMUFFS"; © 2022 by Patricia J. Franz.

Theresa Gaughan: "LIFE JACKET"; © 2022 by Theresa Gaughan.

Xelena González: "DRESS"; © 2022 by Xelena González.

Katey Howes: "OVERALLS"; © 2022 by Katey Howes.

Molly Lorenz: "QUILT"; © 2022 by Molly Lorenz.

Amy Milholland: "HELMET"; © 2022 by Amy Milholland.

Moe Phillips: "JEANS"; © 2022 by Moe Phillips.

Donna JT Smith: "COSTUME"; © 2022 by Donna JT Smith.

Holly Thompson: "YUKATA"; © 2022 by Holly Thompson.

Linda Kulp Trout: "NECKLACE"; © 2022 by Linda Kulp Trout.

Fernanda Valentino: "VISOR"; © 2022 by Fernanda Valentino.

Amy Ludwig VanDerwater: "UNIFORM"; © 2022 by Amy Ludwig VanDerwater.

Padma Venkatraman: "SARI"; © 2022 by Padma Venkatraman.

Jenna Waldman: "BOOTS"; © 2022 by Jenna Waldman.

Vicki Wilke: "GLASSES"; © 2022 by Vicki Wilke.

Matthew Winter: "APRON"; © 2022 by Matthew Winter.

Janet Wong: "T-SHIRT," "ALPHABET CLOTHES"; © 2022 by Janet S. Wong.

Helen Kemp Zax: "PAJAMAS"; © 2022 by Helen Kemp Zax.

ABOUT VARDELL & WONG

Sylvia M. Vardell recently retired as Professor in the School of Library and Information Studies at Texas Woman's University where she taught graduate courses in children's and young adult literature for more than 20 years. Vardell has published extensively, including five books on literature for children as well as over 25 book chapters and 100 journal articles. In 2020, she curated the anthology *A World Full of Poems: Inspiring Poetry for Children*. She also loves cosplay and has several Star Wars costumes she made herself. Learn more about her at SylviaVardell.com.

Janet Wong is a graduate of Yale Law School and a former lawyer. She has written more than 35 books for children on a wide variety of subjects, including chess (*Alex and the Wednesday Chess Club*) and yoga (*TWIST: Yoga Poems*). She is the 2021 winner of the NCTE Excellence in Poetry for Children Award, a lifetime achievement award that is one of the highest honors a children's poet can receive. A few years ago, Janet gathered her son's old T-shirts and had them made into a quilt that reminds her of his many childhood activities, including chess club. Learn more about her at JanetWong.com.

Together, Vardell & Wong are the creative forces behind Pomelo Books.

ABOUT POMELO BOOKS

Pomelo Books is Poetry PLUS. Poetry PLUS play. Poetry PLUS science. Poetry PLUS holidays. Poetry PLUS pets – and more. We make it EASY to share poetry any time of day!

Successful K-12 teachers and administrators build regular "touch points" into their routines to create a safe and engaging learning environment. Poetry can be a powerful tool for offering a shared literary experience in just a few minutes, with both curricular benefits and emotional connections for students at all levels.

Our books in The Poetry Friday Anthology series and the Poetry Friday Power Book series make it easy to use poetry for integrating skills, building language learning, crossing curricular areas, mentoring young writers, promoting critical thinking, fostering social-emotional development, and inviting students to respond creatively.

A shared poetry moment can help build a classroom community filled with kindness, respect, and joy. Learn more at PomeloBooks.com.

OTHER BOOKS BY
VARDELL & WONG

Things We Do

A CBC Hot Off the Press selection

What things do we love to do? In this book you'll find poems from A to Z, featuring action words and photos that will make kids eager to ASK, BEND, CLAP, DANCE, EAT, FLY, GROW, HUG, INVENT, JUMP, KICK, LAUGH, MAKE, NAP, OPEN, PLAY, QUACK, READ, SIGN, TYPE, UNPACK, VISIT, WAVE, X-RAY, YAWN, and ZOOM as you read the playful poems.

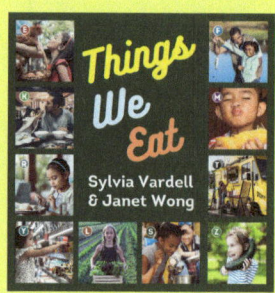

Things We Eat

A POETS.org Summer Books List for Young Readers selection

What things do we love to eat? AVOCADO, BAGEL, COOKIE, DUMPLING, EGG, FISH, GRAPE, HAMBURGER, ICING, JAM, KIMCHI, LETTUCE, MANGO, and lots more! Celebrate favorite foods and introduce new possibilities to try!

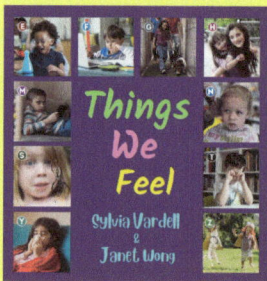

Things We Feel

A CBC Hot Off the Press selection

These poems will help kids talk about feeling AMAZED, BRAVE, CURIOUS, DETERMINED, EXCITED, FRUSTRATED, GRATEFUL, HAPPY, INSPIRED, JEALOUS, KOOKY, LONELY, MAD, NERVOUS, and more. Share the poems to jump-start family talks about mental health at home or in classrooms.

100% of the profits from this "THINGS WE . . . " series will be donated to the IBBY Children in Crisis Fund (IBBY.org).

The Poetry Friday Anthology for Celebrations

ILA Notable Books for a Global Society

This fun book features 156 poems (in both Spanish & English) honoring a wide variety of traditional and non-traditional holidays from all over the world. Also available in a Teacher/Librarian Edition.

"A bubbly and educational bilingual poetry anthology for children." – Kirkus

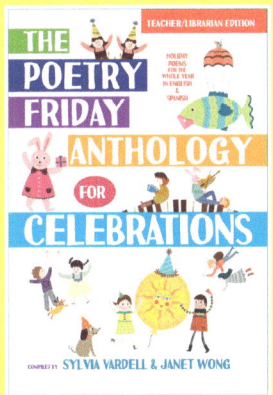

Pet Crazy: A Poetry Friday Power Book

A CBC Hot Off the Press selection

This interactive story – with Hidden Language Skills that engage kids in "playing" with punctuation, spelling, and other basics – features three characters who love spending time with animals. Extensive back matter features resources for helping young people perform, read, write, and try to publish poetry.

"An enthusiastic invitation for kids to celebrate their animal friends through poetry composition." – Kirkus

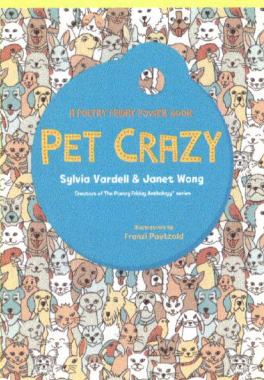

Hop to It: Poems to Get You Moving

A Kids' Book Choice Award "Best Book of Facts" Winner

This anthology of 100 poems by 90 poets gets kids thinking and moving as they use pantomime, sign language, and whole body movements, including deskercise! You'll also find poems on current topics, such as life during a pandemic. Take a 30-second indoor recess whenever you need it!

www.ingramcontent.com/pod-product-compliance
Lightning Source LLC
Chambersburg PA
CBHW042048120526
44592CB00030B/25